COUNTING ZOO ANIMALS

BLACKIE

1 one

lion

2 two

panda

3 three

4 four

giraffe

5 five

polar bear

6 six

monkey

7 seven

elephant

8 eight

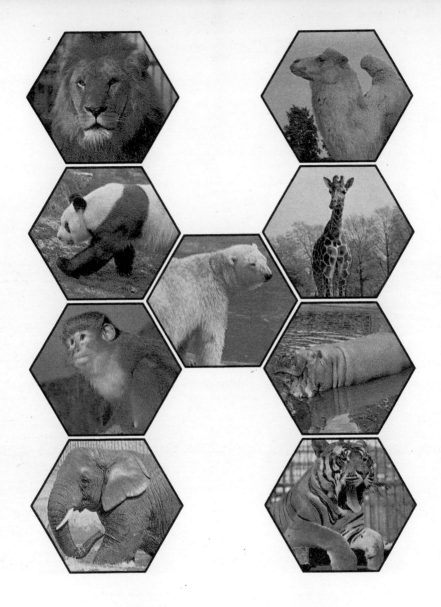

9 nine

tiger

10 ten

gorilla

Blackie & Son Ltd
A Member of the Blackie Group
Furnival House
14-18 High Holborn
London WC1B 6BX

ISBN 0 216 90679 2 hb; 0 216 90675 X pb

All photographs ©Michael Lyster, Zoological Society of London

1   Lion. Mature Male 'Singh'
2   Giant Panda 'An An'
3   Bactrian Camel
4   Giraffe
5   Polar Bear 'Mosa'
6   Talapoin Monkey
7   African Elephant 'Toto'
8   Hippopotamus (Whipsnade Zoo)
9   Tiger 'Vilas'
10 Gorilla 'Guy'

COUNTING
ZOO
ANIMALS

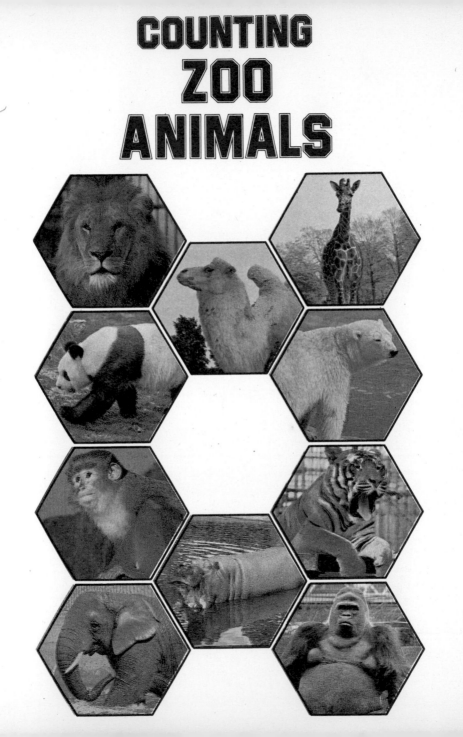